WE, the workingmen of the village of Killiney...

CONAN KENNEDY

MORRIGAN
BOOKS

First published in 2018 by
Morrigan Book Company, Killala, Co. Mayo, Ireland
morriganbooks@gmail.com
© Conan Kennedy, 2017

Origination/Typesetting
shane@goughtypesetting.ie

Cover design
John Hawkins www.jhbd.co.uk

ISBN: 9780907677864

The back story

"There is no doubt that Francis Edward DuBédat (known as Frank), born 1851, was a man with great charm and presence. He had been a brilliant student at Tipperary Grammar School, excelling in mathematics, and by the time he was a young man, brown haired and blue eyed, he had an enviable dose of self assurance."

So wrote his biographer, Maria Wooton, as well indeed she might. DuBédat was a banker and a stockbroker, and we recognise his type immediately from our own times, from our own financial leaders, with their own enviable doses of self assurance.

He was well got. Of Huguenot origins, his family had been Dublin bankers and stockbrokers for many generations. Sometimes up and sometimes down, but mostly up, they prospered mightily, owned fine town and country houses, and all was well in their back yard. They are buried in the trim little Huguenot Cemetery in Dublin's Merrion Row.

But Francis Edward, no, he is buried in South Africa, in the Cape, in a scruffy enough place called Glencairn, overlooking Simonstown Bay. It is a quiet and lonesome spot, typical of many places that shelter dramatic stories in their silence.

DuBédat's career in Ireland had brought him to the top of the family stockbroking business. He married well, enjoyed a lavish lifestyle, and had built himself a fine house in Killiney. Then, of course, and it seems almost inevitably (being overdosed with self assurance) in 1890 he went spectacularly bust. He fled the country, helped on his way, it must be admitted, by one Frederick Kennedy, a solicitor, who gave him a cheque for £500. Yes this must be admitted because that same Frederick Kennedy was the grandfather of this same writer here. Himself a wealthy man, old Frederick was in turn to hit the financial wall some 25 years later.

But all that... another story.

Francis Edward DuBédat vanished. But not for very long. He was tracked down to South Africa, brought back to Ireland, and put on trial. It transpired that his wealth was based on fraud and Ponzi schemes. The revelations made our modern banking scandals look like the details of a minor traffic infringement. Society was convulsed, convulsed. Ok, let's be honest, a *certain* section of society was convulsed. Whether the likes of *the workingmen of the village of Killiney* were that concerned...the jury is still out. How and ever, Frank's own jury in Green Street Courthouse in 1891 didn't stay out long at all. He was sentenced to 12 months with hard labour and seven years penal servitude.

And that...was that?

Not quite.

Frank served four to five years but a mood or feeling gradually grew that he had done enough. Petitions were launched and representations made to the authorities by his family and former business associates. His health had suffered. A few years in the Victorian prison conditions of Mountjoy and then Maryborough (pictured below, now Portlaoise) could do that to a man. Eventually the pressure on the authorities bore fruit, and Frank was released. After a few months staying with friends in the Killiney/Dalkey area he sailed for South Africa again, there to establish a new life which, his health having obviously recovered, lasted for some 25 years. His health in fact recovered to the extent that he took up with one Rosita Martinez, an actress described as 'looking as lovely as if she had stepped out of one of Rosesetti's canvases'. He

became involved in new business enterprises and these brought him back to Europe from time to time. During one of these periods, in 1901, Frank and the lovely Rosita were living in Malahide, as 'man and wife', safely on the other side of Dublin to that of his actual wife and their children in Killiney.

Now about that wife, and Killiney.

In 1872 Frank had married Mary Rosa. He was twenty and she was... I do not know. But I do know that she was daughter of Samuel Waterhouse, a wealthy gold and silver smith with interests in Sheffield, London and in Dublin. Mary Rosa Waterhouse, known as Rosie, had lived in Killiney's *Glenalua House* with her family and, after her marriage, lived in *Glenalua Lodge* nearby. Her father had property interests over large areas in Killiney, owned several houses and had given his daughter away with a dowry of £3000. None of this had stood in the way of Frank's rise to wealth and prominence. By 1889 he had been in a position to buy the house then known as *Stoneleigh,* in Killiney Avenue. He promptly renamed it as *Frankfort*, and equally promptly embarked on spending other people's money on architectural improvements and enhancements and extensions to its lands. This enterprise was obviously intended to be a monument to his success. That house is now known as *Kenah Hill* and the onetime open lands in the vicinity are now *Killiney Heath,* a place of Los Angeles style houses, garish enough monuments to the success of later generations.

After his years of imprisonment, Frank never did not go back to Rosie Waterhouse, staying instead with the new amour, the lovely and exotic Rosita. The first Rosie, the Irish one, she was in fact to die quite young in 1902, by which time Frank (and Rosita) were established back in South Africa. Yes there had been another legal hitch along the way, Frank standing trial again, this time back in London. Further financial shenanigans, of course, but all was resolved. Frank and Rosita then settled permanently in South Africa, living quietly in Kommetjie.

They had one son, Willie.

Frank died in 1919.

Rosita died in Birmingham in England in 1952.

Willie died in Jersey in 1979.

Samuel Waterhouse died in 1905.

Yes, such neat sentences are the bare bones of genealogy, those of us who dabble know them well. With the likes of Francis Edward DuBédat there is no real difficulty in putting flesh upon those bones. Then as now, Celebs are well known, well got, their stories are in the public domain. It's not that their stories or their lives are more important, nor even more interesting than others, it's just that they are available to research, accessible. In fact, when I think, a rare enough occurance these days, when I think about it, the stories of the non-Celebs are actually more interesting, made more interesting by their very unknownness. Is that a word, my proof reader wonders, pencil poised. Unknownness?

No matter, fast forward.

A woman by the name of Mary Bourke from Ballina became President of Ireland in 1990. She had married a Nicholas Robinson. Small world, because this Nicholas Robinson was a descendant of our Samuel Waterhouse above. And thus a President of twentieth century Ireland was related by marriage to a leading fraudster of the nineteenth. And not so many years between them, which shows how fast that things can change, the differences that a few generations can make. And this is where this book is going. I'm interested in a certain cohort of the population of a small village in South County Dublin, a hundred years ago or so. And who they were, and where their descendants are these days, what became of them? It is, if you like, something similar to that tv series, *Who Do You Think You Are?*

But in reverse.

Who Do You Think You Will Be?

Hard to tell. People and families and generations change, and change is unpredictable. Places likewise. Who would have predicted that the Killiney in the view opposite is the place we know today? Yes, that's the road down the hill from the village, Bray in the distance and the Martello Tower in the middle. Making sense then, so to speak, with it's view across the bay. Crowded by houses and trees its location doesn't make sense today.

But what does?

But the workingmen of Killiney?

As mentioned above, when agitation started for the release of DuBédat from Maryborough Prison, numerous petitions were raised from different interests. These were directed to the Lord Lieutenant of Ireland and other influential authorities. Frank's wife Rosa, by then living with her three children in *Willmount House*, one of her father's Killiney properties, she wrote to the Under Secretary for Ireland. Loyalty, albeit misplaced, is admirable in a spouse. Her father himself, Samuel Waterhouse, he got in touch with the head of the General Prisons Board. And a long list of members of the Dublin Stock Exchange presented a 'humble' memorial to *His Excellency The Right Honourable Earl Cadogan, Lord Lieutenant General and General Governor of Ireland.* The humble memorialists *prayed that your excellency will be pleased to commute the remainder* of DuBédat's sentence. Interestingly, several of the humble signatories to this lickspittle effusion bore names well known in Dublin stockbroking circles even up to our own quite recent times. Dudgeon, Bewley, Bloxham, Goodbody. It seems that life in Ireland is a sluggish enough stream, and little changes. Except nowadays our great and good tend to contact Brussels when in search of favours?

No doubt, no doubt at all. Petitions back in the day were what we now call lobbying, which some describe as a multi mega industry of institutionalised corruption, but be that as it may. The particular Petition that interests here does not come from influential and

powerful interests of Victorian Ireland. This one emanates from a different source entirely. Yes it is directed, upwards, via an influential person, but comes not from members of the influential classes.

To the Right Honourable John Morley,
Mount Eagle, Killiney

On behalf of
Mr Frank E. DuBédat.

From the workingmen of Killiney village.

Right Honourable Sir –

*We, the workingmen of the village of Killiney, humbly pray that
you will use your great influence with the Government, to bring about
the release of the above named gentleman from prison. He is now
after serving a long term of imprisonment for misdemeanour and we
sincerely hope that you will see your way towards tempering Justice
with mercy, and restore to his sorrowing family a gentleman who was
ever Kind to the poor, and loved by all. Do this act of mercy, and you
will ever have the gratitude of the undersigned.*

Michael Fanning
Thomas Buggle
Jame Kelly
John Bryan Jnr.
Mark Timmons
John Devine
William Mullen
Patrick Fanning
Peter Mason
John Ryan
John Bryan Snr.
Phelim Redmond
Charles Dignam
William Lambert
Patrick Reilly
Patrick Casey
Charles Hall
James Hall
William Holley
John Byrne
Henry Murnane
Michael Dowd
Christopher Murdock
Daniel Casey
Michael Bryan

Martin Byrne
John Cunniam
James Keily
James Richardson
James Colclough
James Horner
William Fanning
Michael Fitzpatrick
James Ryan
Laurence Reilly
Edward Coyne
Laurence Leary
Phillip Cashion
John Woods
Nicholas Slack
Francis Stack
William Hall
George Hall
Patrick Murdock
Thomas Smyth
John Trevors
Peter Dowd
Patrick Dowd
Andrew Murdock Jnr.
Thomas Prendeville

Thomas Kavanagh
John Cunniam
Michael Quinsey
Patrick Cowper
Thomas Cowan
Daniel Healy
Nicholas Nolan
Kevin Grattan
Thomas Neale
Matthew Redmond
John Stack
James Lalor
Mchael Bryan Jnr.
Thomas Kennedy
Richard Homan
Richard Redmond
John Murdock
Martin Hughes
William Cashion
Thomas Haughton
Thomas Hughes
Dennis Murphy
Andrew Murdock Snr.

And about those 'undersigned'.

It does appear that those names, described in the petition as *undersigned*, are, apparently, nothing of the sort. DuBédat's biographer, Maria Wooton, who unlike this writer has had sight of the original document, she points out that the names are not signed individually, but rather are all writen in the same hand. Be that as it may, the names are there. The actual mechanics of getting them on the paper are lost to history. Of the intermediary, the Right Honourable John Morley of *Mount Eagle*, I know not. Could that be the same Rt Hon who was Chief Secretary for Ireland in the 1890's? Or could he indeed be an ancestor of the Mr Morley the builder who built *Ard Mhuire Park* off Dalkey Avenue in the 1950's, who's eccentric brother lived in a now demolished cottage at the top of Killiney Road, wearing a straw boater in all weathers, watching? Could be, possible. What's definite is that *Mount Eagle* is a grand house in Vico Road, splendid, though in modern times one that seems to feature rather too often in planning and financial controversies.

   Whatever about all that, petition-wise, there can be no doubt that the whole thing was orchestrated by those in charge of the general campaign, and equally no doubt that it may not have been politic for *workingmen* to refuse their names. As becomes clear in the following pages, many of the signatories were actually working directly for the wealthier classes in Killiney, and likely to be living in lodges and cottages owned by their employers. It would hardly have been sensible to have refused their name. Perhaps indeed DuBédat was considered 'a decent man', many Irish rogues do gain that appelation among the generality, and equally perhaps he was generous and charitable. Many Irish rogues are likewise to this day. Be that as it may. The truth is likely that people didn't care much one way or the other. A Petition was going around. Perhaps right there behind the bar of the *Druids Chair Pub* in Killiney.

"Have you signed the Petition?" asks the barman.

"Not yet," says the customer, "give it to me here. And while you're at it... put me on another pint".

This is the way it likely was, though of course that particular exchange might well have occurred down in *The Igo Inn* in Ballybrack. None of that concerns. This is not a sociological analysis of the ins and outs of Killiney affairs in the 1890's. This is a modern writer sitting here with a list of names, and wondering who they were, and about the details of their lives. And what became of them, their children and descendants. On top of which this is a writer sitting here who was actually born not half a mile from Killiney Village, and thus a man with a personal interest. And the purpose of this exercise is to investigate some of his fellow Killiney folks, and learn, and tell.

So let's turn the pages forward.

That always tends to turn the pages back.

Talking of which...below is a sketch of *Cottages in Killiney*. From the earlier part of the 19th century, the artist Henry Brocas died in 1837, so that was years before the days of which I write. But somehow one has the feeling that in the intervening...well...not that much had really really changed.

WE, the workingmen of the village of Killiney...

MICHAEL FANNING? Of him I find no trace.

THOMAS BUGGLE was a 47 year old 'gardener', an occupation classified in the 1901 Census as 'domestic servant'. Yes, I do mean the 1901 Census, which I have had to use to get the basic information on individuals. Remembering that the Petition was prepared in 1896, we calculate five years have passed since Thomas gave his name. He was thus in fact only 42 at petition time, and moving on through the names we may mentally similarly deduct five years from all the ages given in all of this listing below.

Just remember Wordsworth.

Five years have passed, five summers with the length of five long winters.

That'll help.

Born in Kildare, Thomas Buggle was married to Annie from County Down. They lived in Upper Killiney Road with daughter Alice, a dressmaker aged 21 (in 1901 !), and their 18 year old (in 1901 !) son Patrick, who had the same occupation as his father.

JAMES KELLY was a 60 year old 'agricultural labourer living in the Rathmichael townland of Tilly Town. He was also a 40 year old 'labourer' living in Loughlinstown. This is where genealogy gets frustrating. They both lived close to Killiney, and both had the occupations one would expect.

Pick? There are scores of James Kelly's in County Dublin in the Census, but I suspect that one or other of these men was our man. They had similarities. Both were married. James number one could read and write, but his wife Mary, not. That couple had one daughter, Barbara, a 'dressmaker'. James number two, married to Bridget, could not read nor write, but his wife could. They had seven children.

JOHN BRYAN (Jnr) was a 40 year old 'gardener' living in Upper Killiney Road. His wife Mary, née murphy, was also 40, Unlike her husband, she spoke both Irish and English. Their two children were also bilingual. These were William, aged 18, described as a 'clerk', and daughter Mary Ellen, 12, a 'scholar'. Also living in the house was a 17 year old boarder, Michael Durnin, a 'postman'. He also spoke Irish and English but, unlike the family, who had been born in Dublin, he was from County Louth.

The William Bryan mentioned above, though described as a 'clerk' in 1901, was later recorded (1911 Census) as a 'gardener'. He was then working at the house *Mount Eagle* on Vico Road, and it was there he apparantly met Margaret O'Rourke, she working as a cook in *Ayesha Castle* nearby. William joined the Royal Dublin Fusiliers during the First World War, and whilst he was fighting in Europe Margaret worked in London as a clippie on the trams. After the war the couple returned and lived in the lodge of *Ayesha Castle* and later moved to 10 Glenalua Terrace. Somewhere along the way the family seem to have changed the spelling of their surname... a Tommy Brien of this family was clerk at the *Church of St Alphonsus and Columba* in the late 1930s. Descendants of John Bryan (jnr) still live in the Killiney Village area.

MARK TIMMONS (63) was actually the uncle of the householders at the address. These were Patrick Stanley and his wife Geraldine. Patrick (28) is noted as 'Head of family'. Geraldine was 35 at time of Census. Their daughters were Rosaleen and Elizabeth, aged 1 and 3. Uncle Mark put himself down as 'gardener' and Patrick described himself as 'unemployed gardener.'

JOHN DEVINE was 39 year, and also a 'gardener'. (I suspect this was a catch-all word to describe the general outdoors and handyman factotums employed by the big houses in the area.) He was married to Mary Anne (38), he from County Dublin and she from County Wexford. Of their five children, ranging in ages from 2 to 15 years, the older four were born in County Wexford. Their 15 year old son James spoke Irish and English.

WILLIAM MULLEN was a 40 year old 'gardener'. His parents were Christopher Mullen and Catherine, née Masterson. They had lived in Ballybrack. In Killiney William lived with his wife at 1 Hill Cottages. The wife was Sophy (38), a 'laundress'. She had been a Kelly, a family connected to the O'Mahony boatbuilding family in Dún Laoghaire's Patrick Street. ('Kelly' is a well-known name in connection with yacht building in Dún Laoghaire in late Victorian-Edwardian times.) The older son of William and Sophy was also William, and he was a 16 year old 'postal messenger'. A member of the Royal Navy, he was to die aged 34 in World War 1, survived by his wife Mary and 4 children. (60 men from the Killiney-Ballybrack area are recorded as having enlisted in the British forces during the 1st WW). The William Mullen of the Petition himself died aged 80 in 1941, his wife Sophy died in 1952 aged 89.

Among their other children was Jack, born in 1891. He married a Catherine Kelly in 1918. They lived in a gate lodge to the then *Ayesha Castle*, a grand house now known as *Manderley* and as the residence of the singer Enya. That lodge itself is now called *Lios an Uisce*. The couple also lived at 3 Hill Cottages, then afterwards moved to Glasthule. Jack worked for the Customs in Dún Laoghaire Harbour. One of Jack's 4 children was Austin, who married Margie Malone in 1954, that couple having 4 children. Their presentday descendants all mostly live in and around Killiney.

Mullen is a name long standing in the Killiney Village area, an earlier William Mullen being recorded here in Griffith's Valuation of the 1850s. An even earlier record, the map of Thomas Sherrard (1787) shows the Killiney Village site as divided into tenanted plots. Plot 50, consisting of four "cabbins", a garden, field, and meadow, is let to an Andrew Mullen. This amounted to two acres. Another five acres in his holding was "rockey and furry pasture". A second member of the Mullens family of those times was better off. He held twenty-two acres, though "the Hill, rocks and furry pasture" made up seventeen acres of that. The rest was "a croft, arable"

Mullen/Mullin is, in fact, a name so long standing that the unofficial name for Roches Hill was Mullen's Hill. Those of us growing up in the area called it that or, more simply, "The Rocks". The latter may sound simple to the point of simple-minded but is in fact far more correct than 'Roches'. The hill's name has nothing to do with that surname, rather it is derived from the French... *rocques*. Interestingly, the Mullens family name is the only one of the Petition listing that is present on that 1782 Map mentioned above. The ancestors of the others obviously hadn't arrived in the area yet or were impoverished sub-tenants living in "cabbins", or maybe not holding any kind of tenantry at all, just squatting about the place. In those days the Mullens' neighbours around Killiney Village were a P. Darcey (thirty two acres), William Currans (three acres), and Widow Connors, she with six acres. Joseph Sherwood was described as having a "house, offices and fields", on three acres. More substantial residents were Mr John Clarkes, with his twenty three acres, and Mrs Lill, who had twenty acres. Her property seems to have covered most of what is now Ballinclea Heights and Rockfield. Far more substantial was a Humphrey Minchin Esq., he having the seventy-five acres of "Scalpwilliam/Mount Mapas", which was essentially the present day Killiney Hill.

PATRICK FANNING was a 65 year old 'carpenter', his wife, a year older, was a 'mistress'. Interesting, because in modern times in Dublin a female schoolteacher would not generally be married to a 'tradesman'. Though, in rural parts, that situation still persists. Whatever! The Fannings' son William (35) was also a carpenter, and they lived in Killiney Road Upper.

PETER MASON, yet another 'gardener'. He was 48, married to Mary, 41. Their children were Marget, Patrick, and Mary Josephine. All could read and all could write apart from little Josephine. She was only 4. But it was proudly stated on the Census form that she could 'read'. That the parents separated this word out from the question tells us something...they were mobile, upwardly.

JOHN RYAN. A 54 year old 'corn merchant' from County Tipperary. His wife Catherine had been born in County

Longford and the family must've lived in Limerick City at one time, their two sons Ernest and Cecil having been born there. The 'corn merchant' appellation strikes me as stretching the definition of 'workingman' somewhat, particularly as the family ran to a resident 'cook/domestic servant'. She was Mary Colclough, aged 26 and a local girl from County Dublin. No doubt she was connected to James of the same name, we meet him later in this listing.

JOHN BRYAN (Snr) was more than likely the 50 year old 'gardener' of that name living in Killiney Hill Road. He was married to Winifred, a 'laundress'. An unusual name these days, but shared by a travelling woman of my acquaintance whom I support in her daily begging grind on Nassau Street. John and Winnie (I bet he called her that) had 3 children, two of them adults, and I get the impression that parents and adult children were all working for the same large house in the vicinity.

PHELIM REDMOND. Complex, complex. In 1901 Phelim was a widower with an address in Dublin at Royal Canal Bank, Arran Quay electoral area. His daughter Bridget (24) kept house for him, his son William (22) was a postman, and his two younger sons James and George, 20 and 18, were 'Printer's Compositors'. A younger daughter Mary (12) was still at school. All very interesting, but not so interesting in the context of this petition as is the former occupation of Phelim himself. In 1901 he was a 'retired warder in the Prison Service'. And so, we can rightly presume, before his retirement he might have looked after Frank DeBédat in Mountjoy Prison? If so, they must've got on well. And why not, Phelim seems to have had Killiney roots. By 1911 he was actually living in Killiney on the Talbot Road.

No longer a widower, he was living with Johanna, wife, aged 76. Also there was daughter Mary, now 21, but now described as 'adopted daughter'. In later years, the 1920s, a man by the name of Fay Redmond lived in the little house known as Tigín Bán. I do not know the family connections, but instinct tells me that they're there.

CHARLES DIGNAM. I dunno, and yes of course it would be nice if he was related to the Paddy Dignam in *Ulysses*, but he probably wasn't, that being fiction and Charles being real enough to allow his name go forward in this Petition. The only Charles Dignam I could find was living in the Widow Mary Egan's Boarding House in Gardiner Place in Dublin. She was from Galway and he was from Armagh. Other residents included a milliner, a nursemaid, and a young one working in the National Bank. And yes that all does sound rather Joycean, so we'll leave it rest.

WILLIAM LAMBERT was a 47 year old 'General Labourer'. He lived in Uplands with wife Mary and their 5 children. This location needs no explanation, being the hilly areas behind Killiney Village itself. Apparently not an official 'townland', it was the traditional name for the higher areas of Killiney village, roughly centred on the present day Uplands Road, bounded by Cleremont and Glenalua Roads and Roches Hill itself. Another Lambert, John, lived in Kilbogget Townland, an area to the west of Killiney, the border between Killiney and Kilbogget being (more or less) Church Road. Perhaps these Lamberts were related to each other? Almost certain, really, an unusual name. And perhaps both are related to the present day puppetteering family of Monkstown?

PATRICK REILLY A County Meath man, from Dunboyne, he lived with his wife in Killiney, in Uplands Townland. I couldn't establish his occupation. His wife Bridget could not read nor write, but he and the children could. Son Johnny was a 'Railway Porter', and son Willie a 'messenger'. The girl Jenny had 'no employment', and young Sarah was still at school.

PATRICK CASEY. Son of an 86 year old widow Mary Casey living in Ballybrack. Patrick (46) was a bootmaker, unmarried, and his sister Bridget (50) also lived in the household, she too unmarried. Also there with the family were three boarders, all carpenters. These were Thomas (33) and Andrew (25) Kavanagh, and Jeremiah Fitpatrick (29). Mary Casey was originally from County Wexford, her children were born in County Dublin, the Kavanaghs were from County Wicklow, and Fitzpatrick from County Cork.

CHARLES HALL was a 35 year old Roman Catholic 'Slater' from County Wicklow. He lived in Uplands, Killiney with wife Ellen, and their four children aged from 9 to 2. These were James, Richard, William and little Elizabeth, aged 2. The children had all been born in Killiney. It was likely, more than likely, that Charles was son of James, below.

JAMES HALL, a 65 old Wicklowman, lived with wife Margaret, a daughter Susanna, aged 18, plus a niece, 22 year old Sarah Love Laine. (That's what it says!) Also in residence were two 'jarveys' from the Dún Laoghaire area, Patrick Wiley (24) and Christy Geoghegan (22). Hmmnn. If I were a 65 year old Wicklowman I might have second thoughts about letting two jarveys live under the same roof as my young daughter and niece. But that's just me.

WILLIAM HOLLEY seems to have died in the years between adding his name to the 1896 petition and the time of the census of 1901. His family were represented in the latter by his presumed widow Catherine Holley, described as 'housekeeper', she had five small children aged between 9 and 1. One of these, William junior, aged 7 at the time of the census, went on to become the Professional at Killiney Golf Club in the 1920s. Bill, they called him, Bill Holley. And just around that same period one Walter Conan, great-uncle of this present writer, was Captain of the same club. An eccentric Dublin tailor, he invented the Depth Charge. And was Chairman of the old Dalkey Urban Council. Holding the position in 'the national interest'. Naturally.

JOHN BYRNE. A Wicklow man originally, he was 'Assistant Station Master' on the railway. Aged 35, he was married to 30 year old Annie from County Kildare. They had three small sons, John, James and Thomas, aged respectively 6, 5, and 11 months.

HENRY MURNANE. A 33 year old 'Cab & Car Owner', living in the Uplands area of Killiney. He was a member of the Church of Ireland and was married to Roman Catholic Elizabeth, aged 32. In the custom of the times the children took the religion of their respective parents, thus daughters Mary Rosanna and Elizabeth were Roman Catholics, while Henry Bernard (6 months in 1901) was Church of Ireland. Whatever about the appelation 'Cab & Car Owner' in the 1901 Census, the Murnanes also operated as Killiney Village's own local coal merchant, hauling coal up from wholesalers in Dún Laoghaire and selling it to householders.
Luckily enough for the reader, and more importantly for myself, a direct descendant of Henry is Anthony Murnane,

a senior editor with RTÉ News, and thus a man who can put a few facts together.

The full name of Henry's wife was Elizabeth Mary Keenan, and more information on the couple's children and descendants is as follows. Of those mentioned in the Census above, Mary Elizabeth died in 1963. She had married in 1922 and had one child. And her brother Henry Bernard married Ellen Henry, they had no children.

Not mentioned in the 1901 Census, for obvious reasons, was Olive who, born in 1904, married William Kent. That couple went to England and had two children. There was also John Matthew. He was born in 1905, married Mary Fitzgerald and also had two children, one of whom died young. That family lived in Bray. (The Grandson of John Matthew is RTÉ's Anthony, my informant.)

Next in the Henry and Elizabeth Murnane family came Edward, born in 1906 and who, in 1926, was 'killed by a train'. Another child, George, is remembered as having died at birth. Twins came along in 1928. These were Rosanna, who married Charles Musgrave (no children), and Rachel who died young. There was then Elizabeth, also born in 1928, and she married George Thompson, went to England and had two children.

An obituary tells us more.

> Henry Murnane:- a figurehead in Killiney for over half a century, a man known to all for hard and conscientious work, a father who, deprived of his wife in early life, cared for his children and sought their highest welfare. Henry Murnane will be remembered by the parish in particular as a servant of the Church for over forty years. As a boy he rang the bell, and for thirty nine years he was Sexton. The district has lost one of its oldest inhabitants, and the parish a

member who, baptised in Holy Trinity as far back as 1867, loved every stone of it. Happy is the man who at the end of his days on earth can look back in humble thankfulness upon years of faithful service to God and Church, country and home!

And a final detail...

Henry Murnane was the leader of a brass band, in Glasthule.

MICHAEL DOWD, 29 years old, and yet another 'gardener'. Michael was married to Annie, and she was 25. Their daughter was little Winifred, aged 1. A name that popped up earlier, but rarely pops up now. Of these Dowd families I deal with later in the listing, but now might mention that missing O, the O apostrophe, which would turn the name into *O'Dowd*. It's noticeable in these listed names, and indeed in other similar sources from the period, how the O apostrophe is missing from such expected places. Whereas in later years it reappeared. With nationalism? Perhaps. And now frequently in Irish surnames it's going the full journey back into the ancestral language. Just thought I'd mention. And move on.

CHRISTOPHER MURDOCK. Of him? No trace. Yes there was a hardware business in Dún Laoghaire up to the 1980s, and then there was an Irish-born British writer by the name of Iris. She was well up for it, or so I read. But that's irrelevant. Of interest here is whether hardware or literature or even both were in the blood of Christopher... an unknown unknown. Of course both the hardware and litterateur Murdochs went for the ultimate *h* rather than the *k*. Though was Christopher here really a *k* man, one muses? The Census was handwritten, and *h* and *k* are very similar in script, and then the handwriting was read by a machine or transposed by a Canadian company into the internet version...so can we really be sure? Probably not where machines or Canadians are concerned.

DANIEL CASEY. A 'Pensioner of the Royal Irish Constabulary', he was 48, was unmarried and lived in the household of his brother-in-law and sister, Peter and Bridget Mulligan. Peter was a stone mason, and the house was down there in Tilly Town, in nearby Rathmichael. We can only guess, but most likely accurately, that Daniel's connection to Frank DuBédat arose from his former duties as a policeman.

MICHAEL BRYAN. A 'general labourer' living in Ards Cottages in Dún Laoghaire. Aged 40, he was married to Catherine, 38. Of their two children the son James (18) could not read nor write, but their daughter Mary (16), she could.

MARTIN BYRNE. Living in Killiney Road Upper, he was a 'coachman – domestic', which presumably means he was employed to drive the coach of some substantial citizen in the area. Himself, aged 32, and his wife, another Winifred (30), they had five children. These were Mary, Joseph, Winifred, Martin and Patrick, aged from 7 down to 1.

JOHN CUNNIAM A 36 year old 'Wine Porter', he didn't actually live in Killiney in 1901, rather in Dublin's Braithwaite Street. Maybe back in 1896 at the time of the Petition he had lived in the locality, but whatever about that it seems that, one way or t'other, his calling had brought him into contact with Frank DuBédat. I suspect that Frank was on more than nodding terms with those in the hospitality industry. John was married to Bridget, and they had two children, Mary (5) and Catherine (3).

JAMES KEILY. No sign of him pops up anywhere. I suspected first a typo in the listing, and went for James *Kelly* instead. But we already had two James Kellys. So, I dunno. Still no sign of him.

JAMES RICHARDSON. A 34 year old and (you guessed) a 'gardener', he lived with wife Mary in Upper Killiney Road. She was 33, but had not wasted her years, having borne five children aged now from 11 down to 2.

JAMES COLCLOUGH. No trace of him personally, but going by location, and the unusual nature of his name, he was no doubt related to 65 year old Edward Colclough who lived (alone) in Tilly Town, Rathmichael. While it is an uppercrust name, pronounced (by those of us in the know) as Coakley, Edward seems to have left the side down somewhat, being a 'peddlar'. What relationship James and Edward had with Mary Colclough whom we met earlier as servant to John Ryan, unclear, but there must've been some. Maybe James and Mary were children of Edward? Maybe. There's a lot of that word in genealogy.

JAMES HORNER. A 'builder'. He and his large family were 'Brethern', whilst two of the three children living with them and described as 'boarders' were Roman Catholic and Church of Ireland respectively. Those were John Byrne (7) and James Good (5). The third child, George Mansfield, was also a 'Brethern'. It seems the family took in fosters. James (58) and his wife Roseanna (52) had six children of their own. Clara was a dressmaker, James Junior a carpenter, the others were at school. The 'Brethern' are described as a small extremist evangelical group founded in Dublin in 1827. 'Extremist' may be so, but at least they looked after children.

WILLIAM FANNING. A 35 year old carpenter in Killiney Road Upper. His father Patrick (65) shared that trade. The woman of the house was Elizabeth Fanning (66), described as a 'Mistress', presumably of a school. William lived in one of the Hill Cottages, those attractive 'Arts and Crafts' style cottages that lend much to the Killiney character. He could very well have been connected to the untraceable Michael Fanning who headed up this listing. And equally could've been related to the historian Ronan Fanning, who's death is announced as (in 2017) I work on these pages. Strange (I think) to be a dead historian. As if somehow one has found one's rightful home.

MICHAEL FITZPATRICK. Not easy. We do have a 16 year old Michael living over in Cabinteely, but 6 years before this Census he could hardly have been described as a 'workingman' I mention him because, an 'apprentice', he lived in an unusual household, with a single 'barmaid' by the name of Annie Kelly. Also in the household was a 'servant', Katie Cole. Another Michael Fitpatrick was 13, living in some kind of boys' institution over in Kill Avenue. No joy here so.

JAMES RYAN There are dozens (and dozens) of people of this name in County Dublin in 1901. Applying that unerring instinct of mine (which has resulted in such stellar literary success), I'm going for the James Ryan who lived in Dún Laoghaire at 45 Lower Georges Street. He (53) was a widower with the occupation of 'furniture dealer and restorer'. This strikes me as on some button or other. A man like Frank DuBédat would've had a lot of furniture. James Ryan lived with his son Harry (23), also working in the furniture business.

LAURENCE REILLY. A widower, aged 60, Laurence lived with his two daughters in Killiney Road Upper. The older girl Annie (20) was a 'dressmaker', while the young Mary (12) was still at school. That's thirty rather lonely words I've just written there, each one echoing the hard times of the past.

EDWARD COYNE. A 'vanman', living in Dublin City's Gordons Place ? Could be, could be him. No other Coyne, Edward or otherwise, emerges at all. Except of course from my own personal mental filing cabinet of names which does include a John Coyne of Ballina, from whom I buy my car tyres. And where I sometimes get my tracking done. Small world. Same Coyne, the mental filing cabinet further reveals, was nephew of the late Father Liam Swords of Swinford, onetime head honcho in the *Irish College* in Paris, and writer of improving tracts. I was in Frankfurt with him once at the Book Fair. You read it here first.

LAURENCE LEARY. The census reveals just the one solitary Laurence Leary, and he is a 'Gardener', though he is over on the far side of the city in Green Lanes, Clontarf. But bear in mind that five years have passed (with the length of five long winters), passed between the date of the Petition and the date of the 1901 Census. So let's say that Laurence (that's my neck sticking out) *was* in Killiney in 1896, working as a gardener in one of the large houses. But opportunity knocked, and he bettered himself by moving to

Clontarf. And there, aged 40, he lived with his wife Lucy, a year older. They had three children, Thomas (12), Mary (11), and a little Lucy (3). Yes, the theory holds together. The 1911 Census tells us that the same Laurence Leary was now (back!) in Killiney. Not only was he back, his daughter Mary had married a protestant englishman, Charles Edwin Chester. And not only that, she had a one year old child, Lucy Chester. This new family were living with the old, and thus there were now three Lucys in the house in Glenalua. Further investigation reveals that Laurence's son Tom served in the British Army as a Medical Orderly during the 1st WW, that Laurence himself was known as Lar Leary, that he was a gardener in the big house *Illerton*, that his family had originally come from Shanganagh, and that in the 1920's he was to live in Council House 2 on Talbot Road. An aside....Lucy senior was born in Malta. So, had Laurence been a seaman once, or in the Empire's military? Those are questions I would ask, even though the answers might not come..

PHILLIP CASHIN lived and worked in the large household of one Michael Gunn, a 'retired theatrical manager'. Phillip was 33 and, in the same household there was Bessie Cashin (32) she being the cook. They were a married couple. There were five other servants in residence, But then, Mr Gunn was founder of Dublin's Gaiety Theatre, also with interests in London, and had prospered mightily in his career. I could write a lot more about Gunn but he could hardly be described as *a workingman of Killiney*. Even though he had come from humble enough origins, his mother having been a 'burlesque dancer', touring America with an outfit known as the 'British Blondes'. You know yourself.

Ten years after this, in 1911, and some 15 years after the

Petition, Phillip and wife Elizabeth were living in Killiney Village, council tenants in Glenalua Terrace. They had a daughter with them, aged 2, another Elizabeth. Now here's the thing. This little girl grew up to be Bessie Cashion, and is said to have "married a Lord Mayor of Dublin". At time of going to print, I'm still working on this, so far unsuccessfully. If any reader can enlighten, my email box is always open.

JOHN WOODS. A 'stoker on a steamboat' by this name lived in Sweeetman's Avenue in Blackrock, and that hard graft occupation certainly entitles him to the be described as 'workingman'. Whether he was a workingman *of Killiney* or not, another question. Perhaps he just met a mate in a pub who said "hey by the way will you sign this petition, I'm gathering names" ? Perhaps. In any event he was a 50 year old Roman Catholic married to Elizabeth (46), and she was Church of England. No doubt she was English as well, John's stoking on steamboats having brought him to foreign parts and contact with exotic women. Their daughter was Emma (18) also Church of England, as was the custom of the day.

NICHOLAS SLACK was a 60 year old working man, a widower, he lodged in the Uplands house of Rachel Murnane. She (57) was a widow, and had been a nurse. It was a Protestant household, apart from Nicholas, who was Roman Catholic, Yes, we met another Murnane earlier in this listing, Henry, the cab owner, he also living in Uplands. Throw in the query...was he the brother-in-law of Rachel? Most likely.

FRANCIS STACK, we can meet him later in this listing along

with his brother John. That noted, now I'm wondering. These names, Slack and Stack...I'm wondering if *Slack* is a typo error somewhere along the lines, and was our above Nicholas actually Nicholas Stack? And if he was, then was he father of the younger men, John and Francis Stack?

WILLIAM HALL. Aged 39, he was a 'Hackney Car Proprietor' born in County Wicklow in 1860. In 1901 he was living in Uplands with wife Anne, aged 32, and two small children, Rose and Edward, 4 and 2. (And that name Anne Hall reminds me of Woody Allen who used make me laugh, though not any more.)

William was the eldest son of James Hall, mentioned here on page 17, and when James died in 1920, William inherited Hall's Dairy. At that time the cattle and horses associated with this were kept at the end of Talbot Road, the actual dairy being at Hollymount on Glenalua Road. William was to die in the late 1950s, his daughters keeping it on for another ten years but eventually selling the businss to the well known T.E.K. Dairies in Monkstown.

GEORGE HALL. Of him I find so sign, but likely to have been another son of James Hall.

PATRICK MURDOCK. A large family of Murdocks lived in Killiney's Glenalua Road. Apart from Patrick's wife Margaret (40) who was born in County Carlow, they were all County Dubliners. Patrick was 44, and there were six children.

THOMAS SMYTH was a 'general labourer', living over in Dalkey's Ardbrugh Road. He was single, but his married sister Mary Mullen and her two children were living with him. Mullen of course is one of the great Killiney Village names, but no mention of Mary's Mr Mullen in the Census entry.

JOHN TREVORS. Absolutely no mention of him, anywhere in Ireland.

PETER DOWD. A 'general labourer' in Uplands. A member of the family who owned Killiney Hill Dairies. He was married to Sarah Kelly, they had three children at the time of the 1901 Census, Peter, James and Winifred. They lived on the corner of Glenalua and Uplands Roads. (Winifred lived on in that cottage until old age in the 1980s and the corner became known as 'Winnie's Corner'.) The Dowd family of Killiney village are descended from an earlier Peter Dowd, he and his wife Winifred being a couple who settled here in the 1850's. They lived in Stone Cottage on the Claremont Road, and later in a house now known as Tigín Bhán on Uplands Road. Peter and Winifred had twelve children, eight of whom survived, this Peter in the Petition being one of them. Of his older brothers, Hugh had a butcher's shop in Dalkey, and William had a bakery in the same town.

PATRICK DOWD. Another son of Peter and Winifred. At the time of the 1901 Census he was an unmarried 'Dairyman', living with his older sisters in Uplands. Katherine kept the house, and Mary was a 'dairymaid'. Another sister here was Julia, who later opened the Braemor Hotel in Greystones, her husband Richard Gorman having a hackney business in the same town. Patrick, along with his now widowed father Peter, built up the dairy business which came to be known as Killiney Hill Dairies. Their cows were grazed in the fields now known as Ballinclea Heights, as indeed did the cattle of another local dairy, Wilkies. Old Peter was to die by falling off the cliff in Dalkey Quarry, a place where he also grazed his cattle. Son Patrick kept on with the dairy and, later in life, married an Alice O'Grady. She had been the housekeeper in a big house *Ashurst* on Military Road, and he met her whilst delivering the milk. They had three children. Patrick, being a lot older than his wife, died while the children were quite young, and she brought them up. She herself died when they were still in their teens. One of these was another Patrick, known as Paddy Dowd.

On the website of the *Church of St Alphonsus and Columba* in Ballybrack, there are reminiscences of Joan Dowd O'Regan, associated with the Church. She was, the website states, babtised there. Which is a coincidence, because something similar happened to myself in the same church, I being baptised there. The ceremonies 'babtism' and 'baptism' are very alike. She mentions the dairy business, and that they supplied milk to both Dalkey and Ballybrack via horse and cart. She also describes how, back in the day, there were eight shops in Killiney, a Post Office, and a Pub. I myself, of a later generation, only remember three shops. But I do remember the Post Office, my wife's first cousin Una having been the Post Mistress there in recent times. And the Pub, I remember that. Used go there for assignations with my good friend Millie. (Don't tell the wife.)

And so that is some of the story of the Dowd family of Killiney. Only some. But best not omit a mention of Michael Dowd of the same family, he was a co-founder of the Killiney Village Band. Sadly, silence fell when, during the War of Independence, the Black and Tans seized their instruments. Whether as a comment on the quality of the music, or just from their normal nastiness, unclear.

ANDREW MURDOCK Jnr. A single man aged 24, he worked as a 'caretaker', and lived with his widowed mother Ellen (56) in Uplands. Also in the household was his sister, another Ellen (22) a dressmaker. Yes, we seem to be coming across a lot of widows, and dressmakers. Whether Andrew ever married, I do not know. But if he did, he surely left a widow. He became the Park Ranger in Killiney Hill and, some thirty years after signing the DeBédat petition, he fell over a cliff there and was killed.

THOMAS PRENDEVILLE. Yet another Roman Catholic 'Domestic Servant Gardener' living in Killiney Road Upper. Thomas was 40, his wife Mary 27. Both could read and write. Whether they could or ever would produce children? The pages are silent.

THOMAS KAVANAGH, was a 'slater'. He also lived in Uplands along with wife Henrietta. They had three daughters, Margaret, Ellen and (strangely) Eleanor. Thomas senior was 30 in 1901, and his son Thomas junior was then aged 3. A descendant of this family was Noel, a gentle lad. I met him first as a child. I was mooching around Mullen's Hill and he emerged from bracken. We were both about ten. He told me that this was his hill, and I should hop it out of there. We became friends, of sorts. He got a job in

The former Kavanagh family home

Findlaters in Dalkey where he wore a brown shop coat, I went to UCD where I wrote poetry. Later he became a postman. I last met him on Killiney Strand, each with our own kids and separate lives. The only thing in common being that Mullen's Hill belonged to neither of us anymore.

MICHAEL QUINSEY. An unusual surname. No Michael appears in records, though a Quinsey family existed in Clonmore Upper, Co Wexford and, apparantly, a Henry Quinsey of that family was one of those lost in the sinking of the *RMS Leinster* in Dublin Bay in 1918. He was a member of the Royal Irish Regiment.

PATRICK COWPER. A fair enough number of Cowpers around the records, but no Patrick raises his head, neither in Killiney or elsewhere in Ireland. Maybe he emigrated between the time of the Petition and that of the Census? Maybe. Lots of maybes in this genealogical game. Maybe he was even related to the poet of that name, William. Famous in his day, a Heaney of his time, William Cowper died in 1800, and has a window in Westminster Abbey. *God moves in a mysterious way. His wonders to perform, He plants his footsteps in the sea, And rides upon the storm.* That's poetry. And that's the word *Cowper* for me. Apart from the Downs, of course, an area in Rathmines.

THOMAS COWAN Another no-show in Killiney, but in Great Britain Street, now Pearse, there was a lad of this name. Aged 15, he was described as a 'marble mason'. Presumably just an apprentice at that age. He could very well have worked for the Pearse family. Young Thomas, too young to have signed the Petition obviously, he was son of Catherine Cowan (32) head of the family and a 'Dressmaker'. She didn't put herself down as 'widow', instead she put 'married'. So where was Thomas Senior, done a runner? Or was he even the same Thomas Cowan who had once being one of the workingmen of Killiney? I *feel* he was, but I also often feel I'm going to win the Lotto.

DANIEL HEALY was a 'General Labourer' in Uplands. Aged 30 he was married to Annie, she being 34. And yes I've noticed that a seemingly high proportion of our workingmen of Killiney seem to have been wed to slightly older wives, and wonder why is that? No matter, the couple had a rake of children anyay, Mary, Nicholas, James, Annie, Daniel and John, their ages ranging from 9 right down to 5 months. There was also another local Daniel, down in Ballybrack, he being son of a William Healy. From which a leap of genealogical intuition will lead to the conclusion that there was an earlier Daniel, the grandfather.

NICHOLAS NOLAN. A builder in Killiney Road Upper, aged 37, married to Bridget, aged 30. Their nephew Frederick Dowd, aged 10, lived with them, or at least he was there on the day of the Census. We have seen several Dowds in the listing already, Killiney then was obviously a close knit community. The skeins unravelled now, methinks. Also in the Nolan household was a boarder, a girl from the County Clare, Margaret Kelly, aged 21. She was a schoolteacher, and spoke Irish and English.

KEVIN GRATTAN. No sign of him.

THOMAS NEALE. Him neither, though the Census does throw up a lad of that name in St Columba's College in Rathfarnham. Not then and certainly not now an establishment overly familiar with 'the working man'.

MATTHEW REDMOND. A 'Railway Signalman', he lived down in Ballybrack with his brother-in-law, Robert Whelan, a 'Railway Platelayer'. Matthew could read and write, but Robert neither, hence, one reckons, the hierarchy of their employments. Another brother-in-law in the house was Nicholas Whelan, a 'garden labourer', and a sister-in-law Annie Whelan, who had 'no occupation'. Apart from, I reckon, cooking and keeping house for this bunch of buckos.

JOHN STACK, aged 25, lived with his older brother Francis (33) and sister Mary (27). The men worked as 'gardeners'. There were no parents listed in the household in 1901 census. and none were married. John himself spoke Irish and English, his siblings not.

JAMES LALOR. There was a 'master builder' of this name living in Blackrock. Seeing as much of Francis DuBédat's financial problems arose through the over exuberant employment of master builders and the likes we can safely assume that this is our man.

MICHAEL BRYAN. A 'general labourer', he lived in Ards Cottages in Dún Laoghaire. Aged 40, wife Catherine was 38, and their two children were James and Mary.

THOMAS KENNEDY. Annie Kennedy, a 56 year old widow, a 'charwoman', she had a 'labourer' son by name of Thomas. They lived in Victoria Buildings in Blackrock. Our man? Could be. This genealogy thing is far from being an exact science.

RICHARD HOMAN, a 'fisherman', his address given as Vico Road. A member of the Church of Ireland, he lived with his wife, his mother and five sons. His wife 'Lina' was Mary Helena Jahraus. This family do have long roots in the area, a Homan being recorded as one of the skippers of barges transporting lead ore out to ships from the Vico quarries. (These quarries, active from mid 18th century, vaguely opened up again during the railway works a hundred years later.)

A newspaper report in 1877, recording an accident in which 'a lady and gentleman drowned', mentions that the victims had hired a sailing boat from "a man named Homan on Killiney Strand." Being *The Irish Times* of the times, this 'workingman' was given no first name, whilst the victims were noted as Miss Constance Exham and Mr Robert Sullivan. She was of the very grand Exham family who lived in *Courtnafarraige*, and he, of another well-off family, is remembered on a plaque in *Holy Trinity Church*.

A Philip Homan lived in Killiney's Kilmore Avenue in the early 1890's, and so whether he or Richard above were owners of the fatal boat is unknown. What is known is that the family were based for many years at the well-known 'White Cottage' on Killiney Beach, a tearooms, dancing place and base for the hire out of boats. John Rocque's map of 1757 shows this as the location of a 'Bath House', no doubt for use by residents of some of the earlier 'big houses' in the area. As a child, (which wasn't in 1757), I pottered around here in the Homan boats. As a teenager I danced in their dancehall. It's all derelict now. I've a touch of arthritis myself.

RICHARD REDMOND was son of a Phelam Redmond, but not apparently the same Phelim Redmond we met earlier in this listing. He was a 33 year old 'General Labourer', and a boarder in his family house was another signatory we've met along this listing, Laurence Leary, he a gardener.

JOHN MURDOCK was a 'Farm Servant' living in Uplands. His father Christy was 76, and also described as 'Farm Servant'. In the household also was a boarder, William Barnet, (17) yet another 'Farm Servant'. From this distance there doesn't seem too much difference between 'Gardener', 'Servant' and 'Labourer', but there obviously was a careful enough hierarchy.

MARTIN HUGHES was an 81 year old widower of Wexford origins, a 'General Labourer', whilst, in accordance with hierarchy mentioned, his 38 year old son Thomas was a 'Gardener'. Annie, 34 year old daughter, was unmarried.

WILLIAM CASHION was a 'Tramdriver', and where in this he fits, I do not know. But I'm a novelist, and will give it a go. He lived in Dublin in Innisfallen Parade, and he was 30 at the time of the census. But rewind five years or so to the time of the Petition he was 25, and maybe living in Killiney? His likely relatives Philip and Bessie Cashion were certainly in service there in one of the grand houses. And maybe Francis DuBédat saw him as a young man with potential, and had a word in someone's ear, and thus it was that William got a leg up into such sought after employment? Maybe. He was married (certainly) to 31 year old Jane, and they had three children. Joseph (8), Philip (6) and Kathleen (2). A 21 year old 'Clerk' John Ward shared their house as boarder.

THOMAS HAUGHTON. Two Thomas Haughton families are recorded as living in Killiney's Uplands, and I'm doubting already. The first Thomas was a 54 year old Church of Ireland tailor, living with wife, three sons, and one daughter. The wife was Kate, and the children were

Arthur, Ernest, Richard and, the baby of the family, little Margaret. The second Thomas, (Thomas Edward), was a 25 year old postal worker, 'Sorting Clerk and Telegraphist'. He was Church of Ireland also, but had married a Roman Catholic, 22 year old Elizabeth, and they had an infant son. I'm going with the theory...at this stage of the game it's any theory in a storm...the theory that Thomas Edward was he who signed the Petition. Recall again, remind ourselves that all these ages quoted are those in 1901, from the Census, whereas the actual Petition had been raised five years earlier. At that stage Thomas Edward, would have been 20, and might not yet have been the rather upmarket 'Sorting Clerk and Telegraphist', but rather just a young 'workingman' about the place.

We cannot tell.

But what I can personally tell is that when I was a child there was a plumber in Killiney by the name of Haughton, Mr Haughton. Some of my earlier memories are of hearing my mother saying to my father "we better call Mr Haughton"... as we all stared into a blocked lavatory bowl, or watched water pouring out of a burst pipe. My father did not do DIY. This 'Mr Haughton', living in Killiney Village, was obviously a member of the well known Killiney Haughton family. Well known, and very large. I suspect (another theory) that my Mother's Mr Haughton was a descendant of the tailor rather than the telegraphist. This suspicion simply because one of that tailor's sons, Richard, became a 'horticultural engineer', installing greenhouse heating and the likes. And his brother, Arthur, was a 'slater'. That family strike me as being more 'hands on' than the children of the telegraphist might have become. Whatever, the son of that Arthur mentioned, another Arthur, he was also a slater, born in 1903, and his memories of growing up in Killiney are recorded in the Parish History of the *Holy Trinity Church*. Interesting book, put together in 1996 by the then Rector, Cecil Mills. Who buried my father, my father who didn't do DIY.

Small world.

THOMAS HUGHES. A 'Gardener'. He was 29.

DENNIS MURPHY was a 33 year old 'Labourer' living as a boarder in a household at Pidgeon House Road, South Dock, Dublin.

ANDREW MURDOCK SNR. In the five or six years between the Petition and the 1901 Census Andrew Murdock Senior appears to have died. His widow Ellen Murdock kept the house in Uplands, she could not read. Her daughter, also Ellen, was a dressmaker. And son Andrew Murdock Junior was a 'caretaker'. Which reminds...my proofreader John Cully is presently working as a caretaker for a large and empty split-level Los Angeles style hacienda in a housing estate known as *Killiney Heath*. This development is on the lands of "The Park", *Killiney Park House*, a now demolished house owned by the Waterhouse family. It backs on to *Killiney Golf Club* and Mullen's Hill, and lies in the shadow of Killiney Village and of Uplands, and in the shadow too of all the lives that ghost these pages with their passing. Small world.

WE, the workingmen of the village of Killiney...

Of Records, Directories, and Lists of Names.

The word 'workingmen' jumps out to the genealogist, and not in a good way. As far as many of the standard listings go, the records and directories, the workingmen of Killiney and their families may very well have not existed at all. In *Thom's Directories*, the standard brick-sized publications produced each year around those times, and indeed before and after, even up to our own years, very little mention there. In fact only two names of the Petition signatories appear, that of Haughton and Homan. (In 1891 a Philip Homan is shown as living in a house called *Kilmore*.) It is likely no coincidence that both those families were Protestant. Not for any malign intent on leaving out the Catholics, rather that being Protestant they would have somehow been better known to the *nobility, gentry and traders who* filled the pages with their own names. Whatever the reasons and the cause, *Thom's Directories* were no help. The *Registers of Voters* in our own time have moved into some twylight zone and are inaccessible to researchers. Something to do with Freedom of Information. Or rather, the reverse. They are compiled, the reasoning goes, for one purpose, elections. And are certainly not there for the convenience of writers trying to trace the descendants of workingclass Killiney people of 1896. The only such registers that can be accessed have to be fifty years old. Not much use, but some. Looking at the registers from the 1940's one notes that very many of the old families are already dispersed, absent from Killiney. Included in the surnames on our list that do occur is Brian, no doubt a respelling of Bryan. Margaret and William Brian are living at 10 Glenalua Terrace. An Anne Cashion, of no particular address but in Killiney, she appears. A descendant of the young couple William and Anne Cushion in our list ? No doubt. Peter and Sarah Dowd, and Winifred Dowd, they're in Uplands.

Mary Hall is in Hollymount. William and Jane Hall are in 'Killiney', whilst Haughtons abound. Margaret is in Uplands, Elizabeth is in 2 Glenalua Terrace, Ellen is in 'Uplands Road', whilst Richard and Margaret Haughton are in simple old 'Killiney'. There are no shortage of Homans on the Voters' Register either. James and Margaret are at 2 Glenalua Road, Arthur and Dora and (another?) Margaret Homan are at 2 Talbot Road. Then we have a Matthew Mullane, he's in 'Killiney Village'. And we have a Dermot and Mary Mullen at 11 Glenalua Terrace, and Peter Mullen in the exotically named *Venetian Cottage*. And of course we have Rita and William Heffernan of St Abbey's, Killiney.

Heffernan? The observant reader muses, but there is no Heffernan in the list of petitioners. No, exactly. But there is a Rita in my own personal listing of Killiney names. As a child, Rita's shop was right there in the village and was Destination Number One, small boy wise. Ice cream. Toffee bars. All that. A flamboyant woman, Rita, so even at the age of six or seven, I was impressed. Her husband was a carpenter. Was injured in a fall off the scaffolding when they were building the *Holy Child Convent*. Was never the same since. Their daughter ran the Post Office before my wife's first cousin took it on.

I could write a book, if I wasn't already writing this one.

And is there more?

Of course there is, this could've been a longer book. Obviously these *workingmen of Killiney* worked for somebody, and I could've dealt with those wealthier families. Their names were 'great' and their names were 'good', and their surviving houses are listed for architectural preservation. Although mostly forgotten as individuals now, some are remembered in various aspects of Irish history. Nonetheless, forgotten or remembered, those employers were also residents of Killiney, and obviously the neighbours of the *workingmen*, in a sense. But only in a sense. Living in the same locality does not naturally make one a neighbour to the person over the wall. Particularly when one is in a cottage, and the other in a mansion. There is a divide.

Still and all, it would've been a doddle, genealogically, to expand the book to include those on the other side of the high walls. I already know them, in a way. I come from that same class and background but, more importantly, those families are well recorded. Just as their great houses feature in archives, their life stories likewise.

I thought about it.

It definitely would've made a longer book, but a better one?

Eventually I said to hell with it. (Yes that phrase comes easy to me.) I decided that those people in their fine houses already have their place in the sun. To include them here would cast a shadow on the workingmen and their families...just as the mansions of Killiney once cast shadows on the cottages and cabins around.

Not that shadows matter much, particularly. Certainly not now to the people who lived in Killiney in the 1890s. All of them, rich and poor, all now dwell in the same darkness. What's that the poet said? *Sceptre and crown must tumble down and in the dust be equal made... with the poor crooked plough and the spade.*

Yep, that Elizabethan poet James Shirley surely had a way with words. Would that myself and other modern writers had the same.

But we seem to have gotten confused in the intervening centuries. We don't really do darkness very well, and wandering there we tend to shine our lights unfairly. Because yes, sceptre and crown and all that notwithstanding, there does remain an inequality, in life as in death. So my apologies to those Killiney folks unmentioned. Apologies to the shades of William Findlater, The Grocer, and Nathaniel Hone, The Younger, to John Wyse Power, The Editor, (of *The Evening Herald*), and to George Ashlin, The Architect, to William Bewley, the Tea Merchant, and to George Pim, the Haberdasher, and to all the rest, apologies, your books are on another shelf.

It's a wrap

So there we have it, the workingmen of the village of Killiney. Gardeners, labourers, tradesmen, railway workers, a prison warder and a cop.

The surnames are eclectic, a mix, and a few quite strangely unfamiliar. They strike me as having originated in many parts of Ireland, though most of the individuals examined appear themselves to have been born in County Dublin. I do suspect that a fair few of the people met were descendants of the influx of quarry workers to Dalkey in the early 19th century, or of those later in that century who came in for the building of the railway. Certainly few if any of the surnames seem to appear in the earlier records of Killiney. But that's another day's work, for another genealogist. I've done enough, I'll wrap it up.

These workingmen of Killiney are gone to their rewards, and their Killiney, just as mine, is gone. Maybe that's the fate of all who are born on the outskirts of a very large and rapidly expanding city. One's childhood is swallowed up, one's tree-lined lanes are turned to motorway. The world is suddenly divided between those who remember *Rita's Shop* in Killiney Village and those who don't. Change is everywhere. The 59 bus, single decker back in the day, that becomes a double! Like same sex marriage, that is just...not... right. But whatever, ah sure! Memories! The *fifty-niner*, as they used to say. Frank was the driver, Larry the conductor, coughing over cigarettes. They did for him and he was replaced by a younger likely lad of a guy. A younger likely lad of a guy who took up with a girl from one of the big houses opposite *Holy Trinity Church*. Lissom, blonde in my memory, her natural highlights still flash in my brain like symptoms of an oncoming epileptic fit...and she had a pony. The normally placid pipe-smoking Frank would sit fuming over the wheel in Killiney while he waited for conductor and girl to emerge from their assignations in the woods. Strangely, given the context of this book, she married a stockbroker.

The fields where her pony grazed, they're all built over now.

My lips? Sealed.

Today is New Year's Day.

This little book was strictly scheduled (by myself) to be completed yesterday, but circumstances ran it over time. I went to Paris for Christmas. (That *Arc de Triumphe* is much bigger than expected.) The programme slippage is not a major problem, not really. New Year's Day always seems to belong to the previous year anyway. And I won't be getting back to *the novel* until Tuesday. I have a few hours' grace, it's early yet. Very early. A Twitter friend is up feeding her new baby, we exchanged sentences. I didn't tell her that I'm waiting for news from another friend, a real life friend rather than a social media one. That real life friend young woman is waiting for her own baby to die in *Crumlin Children's Hospital*. Yesterday they said it wouldn't last the night. Whether it did or it didn't, right now I have no idea. One thing I do know, however, there is always that particular night for each one of us, the night we will not last.

Every book about life is also about death?

Perhaps.

Between the words on the page, in those blank spaces, is there always another story told, in another language, in some invisible script, a second parallel narrative?

Perhaps. But what so and how so ever, for certain fact we can know that everyone who signed the DuBédat petition is dead, and all of their wives, and their children too. It's a strange feeling, recognising that, scrolling back here through my own pages as I try to reach...a conclusion. A paragraph to lock the door before I leave. I doubt now that I will find it. In my mind now I've moved away from the Killiney of those people. I'm just wandering, vaguely, and wandering through some wilder unKilliney part of Ireland, one of those places where one comes across abandoned settlements, 'famine villages' and the likes. There are tumbledown cottages and cabins there, roofless to the weather, and the lanes and little roads are overgrown. I stand there in the shadow of a gable, reflective, wondering about the inhabitants. There once was a fireplace in this gable, I note, the ope, but the soot is gone from the stones. I remark the large lintol. And that other large stone, a flat one, set in the floor. Much as the soot is gone from the other stones, the footsteps are gone from that stone in the floor. But still I know them there. The barefoot of a child, the pretty of a girl, warming herself, the weary of a working man, resting.

The mind does all this thing and then I say for f's sake Conan Kennedy, get a grip.

Killiney is not an abandoned village. There are no tumbledown cottages and cabins there, roofless to the weather, and no lanes or little roads that crumble overgrown. There are expensive houses, farrowed and balled up to the eyebrows of their eaves. And there's whacking great apartment blocks, one in fact designed by Conan Kennedy. (I hear he's writing books these days). Yep, this place is what it's all about, location location location. This is where you go when you arrive. And it's also an ideal location (location location) from whence to depart, a Killiney address looks good in a death notice in *The Irish Times*. Oh yes, expensive territory nowadays, propertywise. We're talking desirable, out of reach. You'd be hard put to find a gardener, a labourer, a tradesman or a railway worker living here.

But their ghosts?

There for the looking.
